HIS
HIDDEN GRACE

HIS
HIDDEN GRACE

An Essay on Biblical Criticism

ROY A. HARRISVILLE

New York   **ABINGDON PRESS**   Nashville

HIS HIDDEN GRACE

Copyright © 1965 by Abingdon Press

Library of Congress Catalog Card Number: 65-14719

Poem on page 77 is from "For the Time Being," Copyright
1944 by W. H. Auden. Reprinted from *The Collected
Poetry of W. H. Auden,* by permission of Random House,
Inc. and Faber and Faber, Ltd.

Scripture quotations unless otherwise noted are from
the Revised Standard Version of the Bible, copyrighted
1946 and 1952 by the Division of Christian Education,
National Council of Churches, and are used by permission.

SET UP, PRINTED, AND BOUND BY THE
PARTHENON PRESS, AT NASHVILLE,
TENNESSEE, UNITED STATES OF AMERICA

This was written to comfort and teach us all to know how deeply God hides his grace for us and how we should cling, not to our feelings or thoughts about him, but strictly to his Word. . . . For this reason our heart must turn aside from such feelings and with firm faith in God's Word seize and cling to the Yes deep and hidden beneath and beyond the No, just as this woman, and give God his due when he judges us. Then we have won him and caught him in his own words.

—from Luther's sermon on the
Canaanite woman (Matthew 15)

To

Joseph E. Christopherson, M.D.
"A burning and shining lamp"

PREFACE

This brief essay, in essence constituting a series of three lectures delivered at the Mid-winter Convocation of Luther Theological Seminary, St. Paul, Minnesota, in January of 1964, is neither a creation out of nothing nor a piece intended for the experts. The original addressees were members of a "lost generation" of Lutheran clergymen, a majority of whom were trained in a foreign tongue by immigrants representing European views of an earlier era and who now find themselves bewildered by the methods and techniques of the "new theology."

Although the parish pastor furnishes the essay's principal target, its language, I believe, is sufficiently clear to allow the lay reader to grasp the argument and thus better to understand the task confronting every Gospel interpreter. To facilitate his understanding, a glossary of terms has been appended, and, where possible, English translations of foreign works have been cited.

It might be argued that such an essay will enjoy only a limited readership, inasmuch as other, more "indigenous" Protestant groups faced the problems of "lower" and "higher" criticism long years ago. And yet the debates reflected in various official and unofficial denominational publications indicate that the problems raised by the use of critical method are by no means the problems of yesterday. Nor can they ever be, so long as each generation addresses itself seriously to the task of biblical interpretation. Perhaps for this reason then, this essay will have a certain relevance for any student of the Scriptures.

Finally, thanks are due a number of New Testament scholars whose thought has become too much my own any longer to identify, and of whom the argument of this essay will undoubtedly be reminiscent.

Roy A. Harrisville

CONTENTS

ORIGINS 13

TASK 39

WITNESS 62

GLOSSARY OF TERMS 86

NOTES 93

ORIGINS

"Was the world created in six days of twenty-four hours each, or does the creation extend over vast millennia?" "Is the narrative of the Fall saga or factual report?" "Did Moses write the Pentateuch?" "Is the book of Job myth or objective-historical occurrence?" "Was Jesus born of a virgin or was his birth by natural processes of procreation?" "Did he exorcise demons and walk on the water; was he conscious of his Messiahship?" "Who put him to death, the Jews or the Romans?" "Who wrote the Epistle to the Hebrews?" "Is the descent into hell apocryphal?" These questions, and a thousand others like them

13

which deal with the biblical text, its literature, and its history, fall within the province of what is commonly called biblical criticism.

Of late, the role of this theological discipline has become the subject of hot debate, due chiefly to two factors. The first is that the questions with which biblical criticism deals are being put with greater urgency now than previously, and the second is that the discipline itself has assumed a place within the theological curriculum which it did not enjoy heretofore. Whether debate within theological faculties has provoked or aroused discussion among clergy and laity or vice versa may be difficult to determine. At any rate, it is reflected in a hundred different ways, not only in theological texts, but in volumes prepared for Sunday school use, for confirmation instruction, and for post-confirmation youth, in official denominational publications, in formal or informal conferences convened to promote or to stem the tide of discussion. Some pastors suggest to their congregations that the biblical world view requires reinterpretation, and are denounced as heretical by others who suggest that the biblical world view is an object of faith. Some write that a mature, intelligent Christian cannot help but adapt modern evolutionary theory to the biblical account, and are attacked by others for whom the integrity of Jesus and the apostles stands or falls with a literal interpretation of Genesis one to eleven. Theological professors who define "Adam" as generic noun are reproached by others who define "Adam" as proper name. And in midst of all are the questions and queries put by the people, some of whom welcome the emergence of biblical criticism, while others are deeply disturbed and troubled by what appears to spell the opening of an era of skepticism.

In all of this, at least four common reactions or attitudes can be noted. The first is that all this conversation is something new, a fad perpetrated by the chance skepticism of a certain younger element. According to this attitude, biblical criticism takes its position in that age-old struggle between ancients and moderns which characterizes every generation. For the fad to fade, one need merely wait till the moderns become ancient. And indeed, many a critical question has been served up to a congregation by some young hotspur, fresh from theological seminary, who assumes that his people have been walking in darkness till his arrival. In light of such situations, it is understandable why the use of biblical criticism should often be dubbed "modernism," a dangerous term, by the way, inasmuch as it was coined in the Vatican and defined on high Roman Catholic authority as the invasion of that church's sphere of control.

A second reaction or attitude toward biblical criticism is that of indifference. The degree to which this attitude is rampant among us can be noted in the widespread disinterest in biblical texts shared by theologians, pastors, and congregations. For the moment a theologian or pastor is conscious that he teaches or preaches on the basis of texts written in a "dead" language, texts which reflect a history to which a conservative estimate would assign the better part of two thousand years;

the moment he grapples with the problem of determining what those texts intended for their first readers or hearers, and with the even greater problem of interpreting what was intended for men of the past to men here and now, he cannot be indifferent to the questions with which criticism deals. He may be anxious and fearful, or he may be optimistic and hopeful, but he cannot assume that the problems have nothing to do with the task of preaching, and thus treat the discipline as something which time, experience, and maturity will relegate to oblivion.

A third reaction to the emergence of biblical criticism is that of anxiety, anxiety that somehow its use will result in a dissolution of faith. This anxiety may express itself in the inarticulate, hazy suspicion that things once taught and preached, accepted and believed without reservation are now being undermined. Or it may find most articulate and knowledgeable expression, since some who share the attitude are well enough conversant with the use and results of biblical criticism. From out

17

of this attitude arise such questions as these: "What shall we say of the sinlessness and omniscience of Jesus if the Jonah whose sign he gave to an evil and adulterous generation was not a person but a legend? (Matt. 16:4.) If Moses did not write that which Philip stated Moses and the prophets wrote? (John 1:45.) If Ahimelech was high priest when David came out of hiding to eat the bread of the Presence and not Abiathar to whom Jesus referred? (Mark 2:26.) What happens to Paul's great affirmation of the resurrection if that Adam by whom "came death" and in whom "all die" himself neither lived nor died? (I Cor. 15:21-22.) If an epistle was not composed by an apostle, how can it claim to be canonical? What authority remains to the Bible once it is assumed the resurrection accounts cannot be harmonized?"

This attitude, shared by a majority, may issue in a hostility to biblical criticism. It would be comparatively easy to cite American authors who share such hostility, and yet one of the most elo-

quent attacks has been made by an instructor in
philosophy at Berlin, Erwin Reisner:

It is alleged . . . that scientific criticism is justified
because the Word of God has assumed the form of a
servant, . . . because it has humbled itself, . . . and
is for that very reason also subject to human criticism.
Thus critical historical science (it is said) has not
the slightest wish to impugn the Word of God itself,
but is concerned only with a thorough examination
of the human word in which it is clothed. . . . But
is that itself not a dreadful piece of presumption?
If God reveals himself to man under the veil of the
servant-form, then he thereby brings man under
judgment, because owing to his unfitness for God
he could not bear the glorious form.[1]

In Germany such hostility also takes the form
of resistance to a revision of the Luther Bible.
Helmut Echternach, in a piece written on the
limits of theology and published in 1937, insisted
that "the biblical text that is binding for church
and theology and therefore verbally immune from
error is for us the German translation of Martin
Luther in the form prescribed to the church as

text and canon. . . . Whoever ventures the outrageous attempt at textual revision puts himself . . . *extra ecclesiam.*" [2]

It may be that of the three attitudes so far mentioned, the attitude of anxiety is the more informed, since it presupposes at least an inkling, a clue to some of the objects and results of biblical criticism. We shall leave for later the discussion of whether or not that anxiety and its resultant hostility reflect a proper understanding of the methods and limits of that criticism.

If the attitude of anxiety assumes that biblical criticism is inimical to faith, a fourth reaction ought not to be omitted, a reaction not widely shared but nevertheless held by a considerable majority. That is, the attitude that biblical criticism will eventually confirm or at least broaden the basis of our faith. In this connection I am reminded of Werner Keller's popular volume entitled *The Bible As History.*[3] The title of the original German version proposes to demonstrate that the Bible is right after all in matters of historical

20

detail, and its dust jacket carries the seductive note: "Scholars prove the historical truth" (i.e. of the biblical statements) .[4] Examining with burning interest and astonishing zeal the history and archaeology of the ancient orient, and formulating his theses with such confidence that the reader is left with the impression that they deal with positive scientific results, Keller announces that in opposition to that type of skeptical criticism which since the enlightenment "would fain have demolished the Bible altogether," he will prove that the "overwhelming mass of authentic and well-attested evidence now available" agrees with the biblical reports, often down to the smallest detail.[5] The acceptance which Keller's book has found in the Western world—it was first printed in October of 1955 and exceeded the million mark by 1957—is reflective of a certain attitude of optimism in face of the task and methods of biblical criticism.

The purpose of this essay is to provide some answer to these reactions by sketching briefly the origins and development of biblical criticism, by outlining its task and limits, and by exposing its character as "witness" or "confession."

Before proceeding to a discussion of origins and development, however, we pause long enough to lay down a broad definition of biblical criticism. By biblical criticism we mean, in accordance with the original root meaning of that word "criticism" (κρίνειν), a separating out from the gospel message every human element by which it has been handed down and an examination of that element from the standpoint of so-called secular science. Thus the text of the Bible throughout all the centuries of its transmission, the literary integrity of its component parts, and the historical persons, places, and events they record are the proper objects of biblical criticism.

In respect of origins, biblical criticism is as old as the faith itself. When, for example, in his Sermon, Jesus opposed the law and prescriptions of Moses with a "But I say unto you" (Matt. 5:22, 28, 32, 34, 39, 44), and gathered support for his claim by an appeal to the will of God behind the written Scripture, he was engaging in biblical criticism. When he put to the scribes the question, "How can the scribes say that the Christ is the son of David? . . . David himself calls him Lord; so how is he his son?" (Mark 12:35, 37), he was carrying on biblical criticism. The accusation of blasphemy, of acting in concert with dark and evil powers, hurled at Jesus by his enemies, was rooted in their conviction that he had done violence to the biblical texts, had arbitrarily replaced time-honored rules of interpretation with his own, had torn passages out of their proper context, had violated the principle of the unity of Scripture by pitting the Bible against itself, and had forced prophecy into the Procrustean bed of his own self-consciousness. It was this awareness of Jesus' violent discontinuity with the past which awakened doubt in his own witness, who asked, "Are you he who is to come, or shall we look for another?" (Matt. 11:3.) Viewed from a purely historical perspective, Christian faith is the result

23

of a revolution involving the right of biblical criticism.

But it was not until the second century, when the breech between Jewish and Christian communities became permanent, that there emerged a study even slightly approximating what we would call biblical criticism. The most notorious and by far the ablest critic of this period was the "Gnostic," Marcion of Sinope (middle of the second century). Miffed by Jehovah's apparent lack of perfect knowledge, reflected in such questions as "Adam, where are you?" (Gen. 3:9), offended by Jehovah's sanctioning of vindictiveness, by his capricious choices, and by his indulgence in human passion, Marcion concluded that the New Testament authors, in their heat to adapt the Old Testament to Christ, had distorted the Gospel story. The real Christ thus had to be restored, but not till every Jewish taint had been expunged— the Old Testament and its God, and whatever else remained of this taint in the New. The result— Marcion's expurgated edition of the Gospel of

Luke and ten epistles of Paul, in which every
reference to God as Creator, to prophecy, to Jesus
as Messiah, to resurrection, to the human birth
and growth of the Christ was deleted. Now
Marcion's procedure could hardly be termed a
bona fide biblical criticism, since his study was
merely for purposes of providing grist for his
theological mill. Nor was his great opponent,
Tertullian of Carthage (c. 160-220) any more
concerned with matters textual, literary, and historical. Insisting that the limitations of the Old
Testament could be justified as stages appropriate
to man's gradual education toward perfection,
Tertullian nevertheless shared with his contemporaries an almost total lack of any historical
consciousness. Apart from allegorical interpretation which raised the Old Testament to the level
of the New, the fathers in this era scarcely knew
how to proceed. The utterances of the Sermon
on the Mount became the vehicle for the most
abstruse mysteries, and the whole world of Paul,

25

of whom it is said that only Marcion understood him, though he indeed misunderstood him,[6] was abandoned in favor of a moralistic view of the world with its attendant doctrine of the freedom of the will.

These latter remarks may strike the reader as sheer caricature. Yet when all is said and done, the following paragraph from Pseudo-Barnabas (beginning of the second century) is more apropos of the age than those faint glimmerings of historical approach we generally attach to the great names of Origen (185-254), his disciple Dionysius (*c*. 200-264), or Eusebius (*c*. 264-340):

For (scripture) says "and Abraham circumcised from his house eighteen men and three hundred" (Gen. 14:14; 17:23, 27). What, then, was the knowledge given him? Note that he lists first the eighteen, and after a pause the three hundred. The number eighteen is represented by the letter I (ten) and by the letter H (eight) —you have Jesus. And, since the cross was intended to have grace in the T, he says "and three hundred." So in two letters he points to Jesus, and in the other to the cross.[7]

The Middle Ages as well lacked the pre-suppositions for what we would call a historical understanding of primitive Christianity and its sources. When this period was not content with copying commentaries of the fathers, it produced only exegetical monstrosities, an example of which is the Roman curia's establishing of the pope's spiritual and temporal power by its appeal to Luke 22:38, "And they said, 'Look, Lord, here are two swords.' And he said to them, 'It is enough.'" But the period was not all darkness. In the twelfth century, Andrew of St. Victor laid the foundation for a real criticism by comparing Jerome (c. 340-420) and the Vulgate with the Hebrew text and Jewish commentaries. Of Isa. 7:14, for example, "Behold, a young woman shall conceive and bear a son," he did not hesitate to state that the traditional interpretation had little textual basis and that the prophecy, taken literally, spelled deliverance only for the Jews of Isaiah's time. When you recall that this scholar was persuaded to complete his work and to resume his

27

abbacy, and that he was finally buried with all
the trimmings, "the twelfth century," as one
author has put it, "is full of surprises." [8]

The subsequent age of humanism with its con-
cept of reason as criterion of truth returned to
the Greek and Hebrew, and proceeded to interpret the Bible as any other document, aiming at
its simple meaning by an examination of grammar,
style, and logic. The Hebrew grammar of Johannes
Reuchlin—*Rudimenta Linguae Hebraicae* (1506)
—and Erasmus' editions of the New Testament
(second edition, 1519) furnished the Reformers
with their texts, and with qualification the
exegesis of humanism provided the Reformers
with their "formal principle." Though the Reformation itself did not see the birth of criticism as
we know it, Luther was not averse to giving his
critical faculties free reign. Indeed, on occasion he
employed those faculties with abandon sufficient
to elicit the comment that he treated "the time-
honored canonical list of scriptural books inspired
by God with a freedom destructive of all certain-

ty." [9] The reader may be conversant with
Luther's judgments upon various pieces of Old
and New Testaments, with his opinion that
Hebrews was composed of many small tracts; that
James was not apostolic because it contradicted
Paul and neglected the passion and resurrection;
that Jude was a copy of II Peter; and that the
Book of Revelation was too confused, commended
itself overmuch, and did not teach Christ.[10] In
principle, Luther excluded these books from his
canon by leaving them unnumbered in his translation of 1522, giving as his reason his intention
to "stay by the books that offer me Christ bright
and clear." [11] His investigation of individual texts
and passages was no less critical. It struck him as
strange that Matthew should have omitted
Jehoiachin between Josiah and Jechoniah in
Jesus' genealogy (Matt. 1:11; cf. I Chron. 3:15-
16) ; Matt. 19:17 appeared to him as though Christ
would deny his deity; he noted that according
to Mark 15:25 Jesus was crucified at the third
hour and according to John 19:14 at the sixth

hour, suggesting that Mark's copyist had substituted the letter *gamma* (the Greek number 3) for the letter *sigma* (the Greek number 6) since the two were written in almost identical fashion,[12] and on and on. But it must be admitted that Luther's observations, though bordering on discoveries, were only made in passing. Yet by happily seizing upon humanism's insistence on the primacy of the simple sense, and more significantly, by giving his critical faculties their head—and for theological reasons—he not only sowed the seeds of modern criticism for good and all, but also made it possible for his posterity to differ with him in matters critical without abandoning his fundamental theological conviction.

If the Reformation placed the Christian on the threshold of a new science, two factors in the period which followed delayed his entering. The first was the dogmatism of second-generation reformers who conceived as their task the development of a theory which guaranteed to Scripture freedom from contradiction, a theory ultimately to shatter on the elemental. Assuming that the biblical authors were merely the "amanuenses of God," "hands of Christ," "scribes and notaries," "living pens" of the Holy Spirit; their persons were robbed of significance; textual variants in the extant manuscripts were silenced; and the historical character of the biblical languages ignored. Critical questions were left to the Socinians and Arminians. It was inevitable that such a theory should elicit reaction from the side of Catholicism, above all in Richard Simon of the Oratory of Paris (1638-1712), sometimes called the "father" of modern biblical criticism. His freedom in biblical matters no doubt accorded with the Catholic propriety of demonstrating the need for an authority higher than Scripture. At any rate, Simon was the first theologian to assert that Moses could not be the author of all the books assigned to him and that the historical books of the Old Testament could not have been written in the times they describe. It was open rebellion from the side of Protestantism, however, which furnished the second delaying factor—that so-called "natural" explanation of Christianity which we associate with rationalism. Relentlessly inquiring into the origins and life circumstances of the biblical books and their authors, rationalism's appetite for transferring its own ideas and hobbies to the various authors nevertheless rendered its method for the most part subjective, peripheral, and accidental. But if the heyday of rationalism saw little else than an inordinate amount of speculation, its close marked the appearance of one of the more puzzling and devastating pieces of criticism ever produced. The work I have in mind consists of fragments which remained anonymous and unpublished during the author's lifetime. Its conclusions may all be false, but its keenness uncovered the central problems which surround the New Testament witness. The author was discovered to have been Hermann Samuel Reimarus (1694-1768), for forty years professor of oriental languages at the Hamburg Gymnasium. Reimarus proceeded on the assumption that it was the apostles' worldly ambition which induced them to follow the mistaken Jesus, to perpetrate on the world the monstrous fraud that he had risen from the dead by removing the *corpus delicti,* and to establish a community for the purpose of reaping money and power. He then sought to prove how this cruel cunning issued in the hideous distortions by which Jesus was made fulfiller of Old Testament prophecy, by which the magical was introduced into his life, and by which his death was appended with tales of resurrection, ascension, and second coming. Not one of the questions with which present-day criticism deals was left untouched by the "Wolfenbüttel fragments." Let me furnish you a sample of Reimarus' pen. On the Pentecost event reported in Acts 2 he writes:

My gracious! How could upwards of three thousand people have found room there? For these three thousand do not constitute all the persons present. The three thousand were those who "gladly accepted his word and were baptized" (vs. 41), so that there must have been others who did not accept the word of Peter, and besides these the assembled company number a hundred and twenty (Acts 1:15). So we may reckon that there were altogether about four thousand people. Such a number would require a large church. How does Luke contrive to cram them all into this one chamber of the apostles? [13]

The fragments evoked a rash of rebuttals, but the old edifice of scholasticism was crumbling. Its total ruin was signaled in the genius of Ferdinand Christian Baur of Tübingen (1792-1860). Setting out to rid biblical studies of rationalistic extravagances which had driven them from the straight course of research, Baur laid down the axiom by which all further study would proceed, namely, that in no single historical book of the New Testament are the facts of the Gospel history reported in a naked immediacy, that in every instance these facts are set by the Gospel writers within the framework of a particular tendency or point of view.

The only way by which to characterize Baur's century is to call it an explosion. It was this century, the nineteenth, punctuated with such names as Hegel, Schleiermacher, and Kierkegaard, with such events as the construction of the Suez Canal, the Franco-Prussian war, and our own struggle between the States, with the discovery of the X ray and radioactivity, which produced the most revolutionary changes in biblical research. What had been a long time brewing now burst into a flood of studies. Whole libraries of manuscripts and papyruses were discovered, collated, and arranged into families; editions of Hebrew and Greek Testaments were produced in overwhelming abundance; solutions to the problem of the relation between the first three Gospels were proposed which still retain their validity; monographs, commentaries, and series of commentaries on every biblical book were written, in number sufficient to crowd eighteen centuries of work off the shelves; a life-of-Jesus debate commenced, the likes of which the world had never seen; investigation of Hellenistic cults, of Iranian, Babylonian mythology and worship, and of Jewish religion appeared, all requiring another hundred, perhaps two hundred years simply to read and to comprehend. And emerging from the towering mass heaped up by the Baurs and the Bousetts, the Harnacks and the Horts, the Reitzensteins and the Renans, the Sandays and the Schlatters, are those riddles which provide the twentieth-century critic with his reason for existing. "Das wissenschaftliche Jahrhundert," "the scientific century" they call it, and it lies there like some great Moby Dick, taunting and tempting us to sail our frail little craft over, above, about, or alongside it. Name a problem—lexicographical, philological, textual, exegetical, hermeneutical, epistemological, doctrinal, historical—it already existed and enjoyed some kind of solution in the nineteenth century. Our students use Nestle's Greek text, a conflation of three nineteenth-century editions; they struggle to comprehend form-critical method which addresses itself to three basic questions served up by that same century—Jesus' messianic consciousness, the relation between his ethical and eschatological message, and the external circumstances of his career; they wrestle with the hermeneutical problem posed anew in the last century in the essays of Dilthey (1833-1911) and Schleiermacher (1768-1834). At least from one point of view, our own time might be characterized as the Era of the Great Unravelling.

This picture of the origins and development of biblical criticism has been more catapulted than sketched. But it has provided some answer to the first two reactions originally described. To the attitude that we are confronted here with some new thing, the answer is that biblical criticism was heralded early in the church's life, if not in Jesus' own ministry. And to the attitude of indifference we reply that inasmuch as it is the message of the Gospel and its illumination with which biblical criticism deals, it demands our attention.

In what follows, attempt will be made to provide an answer to the attitudes of optimism and anxiety, namely, that it is precisely the non-demonstrability of faith, the nonverifiability of faith which emerges from such criticism, and that since biblical criticism thus belongs to the nature of the Reformation understanding of justification through faith alone, it deserves its freedom.

TASK

Thus far, hasty allusion has been made to the task of biblical criticism. In connection with the broad definition it was stated that the proper objects of that criticism are the text of the Bible throughout all the centuries of its transmission, the literary integrity of its component parts, and the historical persons, places, and events they record. Now the task of biblical criticism must be defined as clearly as possible, and from that definition conclusions drawn which will furnish some answer to the attitudes of anxiety and optimism in face of such research.

Equipped with a nineteen-hundred-year heritage of criticism, some of it consisting merely of hints or clues, as in the case of Andrew of St. Victor or Martin Luther, some of it ragged and dominated by bias, as in the case of the heretic Marcion or the rationalist Reimarus, some of it as keenly developed as a well-honed blade, as with Ferdinand Christian Baur, biblical criticism in our time encounters a fourfold task.

The first is the task of *textual criticism*. We do not possess the Scriptures as they first left the hands of their authors. We enjoy them for the most part at anywhere from one to three hundred years' remove from their originals. Nor did the biblical texts become fixed until their acceptance into the Christian canon. For this reason, the restoration of those texts to a point most closely approximating their "autographs" is of a piece with biblical criticism. The fact that there are close to five thousand extant manuscripts of the New Testament alone—to say nothing of the one hundred thousand quotations or allusions in the ancient fathers of the church—and that in part, the library of the New Testament underwent some four or five hundred years of copying before universal acceptance led to any fixing of texts, indicates the scope of the task.

To cite an analogy, if you were to turn in your Revised Standard Version of the Bible to Romans, chapter five, you would see that to the text of verse one—"Therefore, since we are justified by faith, we have peace with God"—is affixed the note, "Other ancient authorities read 'let us' [have peace with God]." Now which is the correct reading? Such a question cannot be answered by merely pointing to the oldest Greek manuscript available on Rom. 5:1. A quotation of that passage by the arch-heretic Marcion could be more accurate, provided it rested on a manuscript tradition older than the one available. (The oldest book in my library is dated 1704, but it is not a first edition, perhaps not even the copy of a first edition.) This problem immediately hurls us into questions of textual history. That is, we must now arrange all our manuscripts on Rom. 5:1 into groups or "families," must determine which of them hark back to the earliest possible period, and on this basis seek to fix the proper reading. Now it just so happens that from this investigation Marcion's version emerges as the best attested. Up to this point, at least, the reading "let us have peace with God" gets the nod. This is what the Bible says, as nearly as we can determine. Up to this point, at least, all your Reformation sermons are for burning. Your suspicion is aroused, however. You recall or examine other sections in which the author draws similar consequences for the believer's existence. You ask yourself what real-life situation in the Roman community might have elicited the one or the other reading. You toy with the possibility that the letter was not written by the man whose name it bears and speculate on the type of reading you might encounter if the epistle were written by another. You draw your conclusions. To whatever degree you seriously indulge in such reflection, to that degree you are engaging in *literary*

criticism—the second major task of biblical research. For it is impossible that criticism of the
text should be made without a knowledge of the
style, habits of thought, and circumstances of the
author whose text you are to restore. Your reflection on Rom. 5:1 may lead you to conclude with
many a reputable scholar that the reading in the
appended note contradicts the whole temper of
the letter. You may even go on to speculate a bit
as to how that additional reading ever crept into
the body of ancient witnesses, and may conclude
that while Paul was dictating the letter, his secre-
tary confused a long with a short "o." All this
conjured up by one tiny Greek vowel!

To continue our analogy, at this point you attempt arranging this little verse within an ordered whole. You consider it in relation to the
rest of the chapter, to the entire epistle, to all the
writings of Paul (and this will give you pause, for
not all the writings attributed to Paul are believed
to have been written by him), and finally to the
rest of the New Testament library. You recall that

Socrates, Plato, and the Stoics talked of righteousness, and you compare their ideas with Paul's. You reflect on the concepts "righteousness" and "justification" as used in religions contemporaneous with primitive Christianity. You recall the photograph of an alabaster frieze once seen in a volume on archaeology. There stands the devotee in a pit beneath an iron grate; the blood of the bull or goat above him drips down upon his head and shoulders; beneath, the inscription reads, "Justified! Reborn to all eternity!" You ask yourself, "How did Paul come to believe this of *Jesus*? How did his readers manage to live as though all this were true of *Jesus*?" Such questions belong to *historical criticism*—the third task of biblical research. For if the textual inevitably leads to the literary question, without the historical question, without setting the literature into an ordered whole, the critic has done nothing beyond adding a few more footnotes on dates and authorship already crowding our shelves. Now the textual, literary, and historical questions raised by Rom.

5:1 are much simpler than those raised, for example, by the synoptic accounts of the feeding miracle, in which the condition of the texts is a welter of confusion by comparison. And yet precisely the same method prevails.

With the approach you have made thus far toward an exposition of Rom. 5:1, one thing ought to have been crystal clear to you. You have used your wits. No doubt, you bowed your head at the outset, asking God to enlighten your mind for what you were about to do, but you did not assume you would get the answers to your questions in a vision or ecstasy. You expected to sweat it out. In other words, you proceeded to your critical work precisely as you would interpret a line from Shakespeare or Tennessee Williams. You were not in possession of any specifically Christian or "spiritual" method of fulfilling your task. You had no option but to take your place with every other historian, to pass through the same dangers, difficulties, and successes as he. In method, at least, you did not consider your text

45

after the analogy of Jesus Christ. That is, you did not assume that Rom. 5:1, in spite of its human character, somehow stood outside the context of world literature with all its dilemmas and contradictions. You did not secure to your passage a sphere peculiar to itself, an unassailable realm which exists above or alongside other literature, a realm to be assessed by totally different criteria than any other literature. You may hold such an idea in theory, but if you took any of the steps in the approach outlined, they gave that theory the lie.

It is time now to drop the analogy. You may never go to your texts in this fashion for a whole family of reasons, but you may nevertheless be troubled by those who do. For is there not a danger that with the use of critical-historical method the very substance of theology, the uniqueness of the revelation of God in Jesus Christ, will be destroyed? Do we not require some final, absolute doctrinal authority respecting Scripture, a Syllabus of Errors perhaps, or at least an antimodernist oath, an ecclesiastically authorized theology, and the enforcement of one clear, un-equivocal position which will make forever im-possible the ruthlessness of a Marcion or a Reimarus? Ought we not take our stand with that German philosophy instructor or with Helmut Echternach? Or are we troubled about nothing? Ought we to face the inevitable fires of biblical criticism optimistically, convinced with Werner Keller that every biblical utterance, every event recorded, every person described, every jot and tittle will ultimately have its vindication in philology, lexicography, history, comparative re-ligion, and archaeology? Ought we to believe that what may appear to be shaky today will prove to-morrow to be stable after all?

The answer to these questions is that *in prin-ciple* biblical criticism can neither destroy nor support faith—because of the nature of faith. Biblical criticism limits itself to a verification of the verifiable, to a demonstration of the demon-strable—facts, objectifiable history, occurrences, whatever can be known or ascertained by dint of sheer logic and mental effort. Faith, on the other hand, is the appropriation of an event which includes not merely fact but its interpretation, not merely the historical but its significance, not merely occurrence but its meaning. This melting together of the word of the cross and the word about the cross into one word, one event to be believed and obeyed occurs on every page of Scripture. In Rom. 4:25, for example, Paul not merely announces that Jesus was crucified and raised, but that he was "put to death *for our trespasses* and raised *for our justification.*" Biblical criticism deals only with the first half of this sentence, but faith embraces the whole. Indeed, if faith embraced merely the half, the fact of death and resurrection, it would not be faith at all but mere assent to a proposition. But this means that faith's specific and peculiar character is derived from appropriation of the significance of the fact and not that fact itself. The Reformers clearly understood that it is not the record of something

which has taken place, however verifiable, but
rather a witness to the meaning of what has taken
place which offers itself to faith. In his exposition
of the Gospels, Luther never tired of emphasizing
the insufficiency of a mere *fides historica,* that is,
of a faith construed as assent to brute facts. Even
Satan, he wrote, can believe that Christ was born
of the Virgin Mary and was laid in the crib at
Bethlehem; even the damned believe this story.
The important thing is that we receive the "to
you" of Luke 2:11 in faith.[1] For whoever cannot
believe that Christ was born for him, for him
Christ was born in vain.[2] The fact of the Virgin
birth alone is not decisive. Accordingly, Angelus
Silesius (1624-77) put the Christmas word in
this fashion: "Wär' Christus tausendmal in Bethlehem geboren und nicht in mir—ich wäre doch
verloren" ("I were lost, were Christ a thousand
times in Bethlehem born, and not in me").
" 'Faith' does not signify merely the knowledge
of the history . . . but signifies a faith which be-
lieves, not merely the history, but also the effect of

the history," states the Augsburg Confession, Article XX. And again, Article XXIV reads, "Nor is it enough only to remember the history; for this also the Jews and the ungodly men remember." Melanchthon puts his case so strongly he gives the impression of cutting justifying faith completely loose from *fides historica*. In his *Loci* on justification and faith he writes:

This sophistic faith which they first call "formless" and then "acquired," and by which the impious give assent to the evangelical histories much as we are accustomed to do in the case of the histories of Livy and Salust, is no faith at all but is merely opinion. . . . Scripture most simply uses the word faith; and that Parisian quality cannot be called faith, which they say even the impious and the despisers of God possess. . . . faith is nothing other than reliance upon the divine mercy promised in Christ (regardless of the sign involved) .[3]

If it is true that faith receives its character as faith from trust in the witness to the meaning of God's saving act in Christ, how can it be destroyed or supported by a study or criticism of that which in the final analysis does not constitute faith as faith? To make things clearer, let me give a further example. Since the nineteenth century, there has been continual debate among biblical critics respecting Jesus' messianic consciousness. Did he or did he not consider himself the Messiah of Old Testament hope and prophecy? Are those biblical sections in which he affirms his Messiahship to be attributed to the subsequent faith and confession of the primitive Christian community, or do they represent the oldest stratum of the Gospel tradition? Sixty-four years ago, Wilhelm Wrede (1859-1906) insisted that Jesus did not acknowledge himself to be Messiah, that those utterances in which he appears to do so are the peculiar contribution of the Gospel writer.[4] Later, Albert Schweitzer (1875-) insisted that Jesus did indeed acknowledge himself to be Messiah, though in reality he was mistaken and gave vent to his heartbreak in that pitiful cry, "My God, my God, why hast Thou forsaken me?" [5] After performing considerable surgery on both hypotheses, modern New Testament criticism has followed either Wrede's or Schweitzer's leading, the majority of critics siding with Wrede. We let Ernst Käsemann of the theological faculty at Tübingen sum up for that majority:

The term "Son of Man" might well reflect the Christology and apocalyptic of post-Easter Christianity. From there, it might well have penetrated the tradition about Jesus. . . . If . . . Jesus never expressly raised claim to Messiahship, that . . . would be extraordinarily characteristic of him. In that case he would be as different from late-Jewish expectation as he was from the preaching of his own community. He then would not have drawn a picture of the future, but would have done what was necessary in the immediate present and would have placed not his person but his task at the mid-point of his preaching.[6]

Now, assuming that this is the case, how does this historical-critical denial of Jesus' messianic consciousness constitute a denial that he is Messiah and Word of God for us? Is it not one thing to be conscious of messiahship, to claim that messiahship publicly, and quite another to be in very truth the Messiah? If not, then indeed, the critical denial of Jesus' messianic consciousness is a removal of the foundation of our faith. But in face of such a deduction, I can only say that my faith can neither take its stance from the negations of criticism, nor, indeed, in opposition to that criticism. For then it would not be faith, but something else.

This is not to say that in *actual practice* biblical criticism cannot be destructive of faith, or that faith cannot take comfort from the results of biblical research. In his autobiography the famous romanticist biographer of Jesus, and one-time theological student Ernest Renan (1823-92) claimed that he lost his faith for reasons connected with the study of philosophy and biblical criticism.[7] And who would care to cite the innumerable examples of persons known to us who have shared the same fate? On the other hand, as already noted, the inventory of Werner Keller's *The Bible As History* tells the story of hundreds who gather support for their faith from the archaeologist's spade. All this is not surprising, inasmuch as disinterested, diffident people do not engage in biblical criticism. But again, the answer to such postures is that faith, while intensely interested in the objects of historical critical work, cannot be dependent upon its results. Not only because of the nature of faith, but also because of the nature of that criticism itself.

First of all, the results of biblical criticism are a shifting sand. You have just learned something of the debate regarding Jesus' messianic consciousness. Reputable scholars take their position on both sides of the fence. Today the majority follow Wrede, with qualification. What will they do tomorrow? Yesterday, the majority doubted the integrity of the Fourth Gospel in the matter of historical details. Today, the majority of critics is inclined to place a greater amount of confidence in the evangelist regarding such details. Who knows what will happen tomorrow? Yesterday, four epistles were established beyond reasonable doubt as coming from the hand of Paul—Romans, Galatians, First and Second Corinthians. Today, only Ephesians and the Pastoral Letters lie in doubt. And tomorrow? Theological students occasionally ask, "What if the resurrection were disproved? What then?" The answer is that the resurrection has already been disproved, masterfully disproved, at least to the satisfaction of whole companies of men and women two hundred, one hundred years ago, by Reimarus, by David Friedrich Strauss (1808-74). Yet the majority of critics today insist with Martin Dibelius (1883-1947) that "something must have happened," something which not only produced a "complete reversal of the disciples' attitude following the crucifixion," but which also "enabled them to engage in renewed activity and to found the primitive Christian community." [8] Tomorrow, in the hand of the critic, that "something" may turn into a nothing again, or it may turn into a line from the Nicene Creed.

If the results of biblical criticism are a shifting

sand, the reason is that the views on the basis of which the critics do their work are sufficiently subjective as to produce such varied results. No genuine critical study can be pursued apart from hypotheses or basic points of view, but it is precisely at the point where the critic chooses the hypothesis from which he will proceed that his own tastes and concerns play a major role, first, in the framing of his hypothesis, then in the selection of material by which he hopes to prove it. It is humanly impossible that his results should not in some way be informed by his own subjectivity. In fact, without subjectivity, without appetite and hope, historical study is inconceivable. There is no depending upon the disinterested. Love for the truth is never a diffident affection. But for that very reason, all historiography, and biblical criticism which has shared with it a parallel fate, can only demonstrate probabilities. The more cautious the critic, the more he is aware of the presence of his own specific point of view, his own limitations, sympathies and antipathies, the greater the probability—but probabilities cannot catapult us into faith. As the gloomy Dane once put it: "Faith is by no means partial to probability; to make such an assertion about faith is to slander it." [9]

But that which ultimately draws the great question mark over all textual, literary, and historical study of the Bible is the Bible itself. Not only do the biblical authors themselves share specific points of view, specific theologies which so dominate the selection and arrangement of their material as to render the task of separating fact from interpretation virtually superhuman; not only is the Bible written from faith—it is also written *for* faith. To return to our analogy for one last time, once you have established the condition of the text of Rom. 5:1, determined its literary integrity, and set it within an ordered whole, your work has been only half completed! For it is not enough to make clear what those words—"Therefore . . . we have peace with God"—intended for their author and original audience. Their character is such that they demand to be actualized, made con-

temporary, heard and understood and believed
here and now! Far from a mere opening of the
Bible to Rom. 5:1 and putting to it the question,
"What does it mean to me?" or, "To what recent
occurrence in my town can I relate it?"—a practice
which characterizes much of the treatment of biblical texts, a treatment infinitely more subjective,
more arbitrary, and ultimately more destructive of
faith than the most radical criticism because of its
total unawareness of the self, its tastes, and its
hopes—a genuine actualizing of the text demands
translation, interpretation. Rom. 5:1, in its present form, is unintelligible to your hearer, beyond
conjuring up those vague, mystical feelings as-
sociated with churches and altars and pulpits. The
world view, the entire context of thought within
which this little verse lies as in a manger requires
translation into a world view of which Copernicus
and Einstein and Edward Teller have made us the
inheritors. The preacher must get out of Palestine.
This task of actualizing, of making contemporary,
sometimes defined as "theological exegesis," re-

quiring for its fulfillment a knowledge of what and how men and women think, is the hardest, the bitterest of them all, and the question as to the proper balance between this actualizing and the steps which precede it will occupy biblical critics, pastors, and teachers long after we have turned to sod. But it can never be escaped, for the Bible is never the Word of God quantitatively. The Christ who proclaims himself in it intends further to be proclaimed. There is no possibility of leaning on a dogma or theory of Scripture which can free the preacher from the agony of making the Bible contemporary. The Word of God is an event which begins with the text and culminates in the preaching, in preaching that is heard and understood.

For the recognition of this truth in our own time we are indebted to the catastrophe of the First World War and the cultural and scientific crisis which it brought about, which echoed the demand for inquiry into the "stuff" or "matter" of the biblical texts. The decisive thrust came from outside the biblical disciplines. In 1919, the Swiss pastor Karl Barth (1886-   ), pupil of Adolf von Harnack and associate editor of the most influential organ of free Protestantism, published a commentary on Romans which originated in the distress of the preacher who was required to expound the biblical text but could not. Here are the opening lines in Barth's preface to his first edition:

Paul, as a child of his age, addressed his contemporaries. It is, however, far more important that, as Prophet and Apostle of the Kingdom of God, he veritably speaks to all men of every age. The differences between then and now, there and here, no doubt require careful investigation and consideration. . . . The historical-critical method of biblical investigation has its rightful place: it is concerned with the preparation of the intelligence—and this can never be superfluous. . . . Nevertheless, my whole energy of interpreting has been expended in an endeavour to see through and beyond history into the spirit of the Bible. . . . What was once of grave importance—and not merely crotchety and incidental —stands in direct connection with that ancient gravity. If we rightly understand ourselves, our prob-

lems are the problems of Paul; and if we be en-
lightened by the brightness of his answers, those
answers must be ours.[10]

It is thus not only the nature of faith or the
nature of biblical criticism, however ruthless or
gentle the critic, however poorly or grandly
equipped, but the object of the critic's research
which ultimately calls his criticism into question.
It is this object which renders biblical criticism
with its division of fact from interpretation an
abstraction and relegates it to the position of an
ancillary, a subordinate undertaking. It is what
the Bible wills and intends which makes impossible any anxiety or optimism in the face of biblical
criticism. For Scripture begins where biblical criticism leaves off—with the call to faith.

WITNESS

In partial answer to the attitudes of anxiety and optimism in face of biblical criticism, it was stated that that criticism can neither destroy nor support faith; first of all, because of the nature of faith which derives its character not from assent to data, but from an appropriation of their meaning; and secondly, because of the nature of biblical criticism whose results are a shifting sand. Finally, it was stated that faith can neither be destroyed nor supported by biblical criticism because the object of such criticism, the Bible itself, is not merely a book of yesterday, but a message demanding further to be proclaimed, to be heard and understood, rejected or believed here and now.

In light of this ought we to bother our heads with criticism? If, as Barth writes, the task of preaching and interpreting is to "stand with nothing before me but the enigma of the matter; till the document seems hardly to exist as a document; till I have almost forgotten that I am not its author; till I know the author so well that I allow him to speak in my name and am even able to speak in his name myself," [1] does not the church's occupation with problems textual, literary, and historical spell a return to those dry and superficial investigations with which a whole century of commentaries is filled? Listen to one of them picked at random on the Christmas Gospel:

Glory to God *in the highest,*
And *on earth* peace among men of His good will.
"Glory" balances "peace," "in the highest" balances "on earth," "to God" balances "among men of His good will." This exact correlation between the parts is lost in the common triple arrangement; which has the further awkwardness of having the second member introduced by a conjunction, while the third is not,

and of making the second and third members tautological.[2]

How have I been addressed, judged, condemned, and summoned to peace with God by something which appears to be little more than the "first draft of a paraphrase of the text"? [3] And if, though not in principle, yet surely in actual fact, men and women are troubled by the questions with which biblical criticism deals—whether disturbed by the questions themselves, as was Ernest Renan, or put on the defensive with its answers, as is Werner Keller—ought we not to abandon the entire enterprise? The better part of this essay has been spent in sketching the origins and development, the task and limits of biblical criticism, and I wager that though you may be interested, everything boils down to the one little question—"Why bother?"

The answer, first of all, is that the preacher cannot get out of Palestine until he has been there. He cannot struggle with actualizing, making contemporary his text, until he has wrestled with the textual, literary, and historical problems. It is true, two days before his death, Luther emphasized the absolute necessity of actualizing the Scriptures, and on the basis of one's own experience. He wrote:

No one can understand Virgil's Bucolics or Georgics unless he has spent five years as a shepherd or farmer. No one (I contend) can understand Cicero's letters unless he has been employed for twenty years in some kind of office in the republic. No one knows whether he has tasted Holy Scripture sufficiently, unless, with the prophets, he has led the churches for a hundred years. . . . We are beggars. That is for sure.[4]

But the same Luther had underscored just as masterfully the fact that such actualization or making contemporary does not proceed *beyond* the letter, but *through* it. In a sermon on I Cor. 15:1 ff., delivered the afternoon of August 11, 1532, he said:

In this passage you hear how Saint Paul cites Scripture as his strongest evidence and shows that there is no basis for preserving our doctrine and faith beyond

65

the bodily or scriptural word contained in letters and orally preached by him or by others. For here it is clearly Scripture, Scripture, Scripture! Now he is not a vain Spirit of whom they drivel that the Spirit alone must accomplish it, that the Scripture is a dead letter and cannot give life. But it is also stated that though the letter of itself does not give life, it still must be present, heard or received, that through it the Holy Ghost must work in the heart, and that through that word and in that word the heart must be kept in faith against the devil and all temptation. So do not boast overmuch of the Spirit when you do not have the visible, external word.[5]

In other words, without the letter, without that kind of understanding which biblical criticism has for its object, subjectivity, personal experience, theological exegesis—all run rampant. To illustrate: Commenting on the women's question, "Who will roll away the stone for us from the door of the tomb?" the expositor of Mark's Easter narrative in *The Interpreter's Bible* writes:

The stone was too heavy for them. There it loomed before their minds, immovable.
    It is a type of thinking that so easily besets us, large-

ly because more than we realize we have shared in the secular temper about us. In spite of our belief in God we tend to look out on the world, or on particularly difficult situations, as though only mundane factors were at work. "Here is this mountainous stone. When will it ever get rolled away?" So men's minds have run. And the only answer is "Never," as long as they think only of earthly powers.[6]

Now this comment can hardly be cited as an example of biblical interpretation which has run amok. And yet beyond finding in the event of Easter its occasion, what is to prevent these words from being applied to scores of other biblical narratives—the narrative of the storm, say, with its question, "Teacher, do you not care if we perish?" (Mark 4:38) or that of the feeding and its question, "How can one feed these men with bread here in the desert?" (Mark 8:4) or that of the rich young ruler with its final query, "Then who can be saved?" (Mark 10:26). Has the women's question no meaning of its own, in a context all its own, a context shatteringly unlike that of the others? If it has, then how does the comment just cited differ qualitatively from the so-called "spiritual" exegesis of the Middle Ages, for which the literal sense served largely for the instruction of babes? And further, what right does the narrative itself give for assuming that the women's question was uttered from a way of looking at the world "as though only mundane factors were at work"? From one point of view, their subsequent fright and silence could be laid at the door of their credulity rather than at that of their disbelief. Truth may be beautifully uttered, made bitingly relevant; but without concentration on the particularity of words in their context, what the Bible intends further to be proclaimed—a quite particular and concrete Word—will never be heard. Theological exposition cannot be given its head; it requires the bit and bridle of biblical criticism.

Secondly, we bother our heads with biblical criticism, for, though unable to destroy or support faith, it nevertheless points faith to its proper sphere. It was stated earlier that biblical criticism inevitably collides with and is called into question by its object—a Word to be heard and to be believed. From a purely historical standpoint, the church's present preoccupation with the "stuff" of the Scripture and its contemporizing, and the resultant discussion of biblical interpretation which promises to turn the theological curriculum upside down, would never have come about if there had not been prior application to the tedious business of textual, literary, and historical criticism. For through these steps the collision occurs. But more than this, biblical criticism witnesses to faith's proper sphere by putting to it the question as to whether or not it will be bound by a specific picture of history or by a specific faith. In other words, if faith means to embrace the meaning of what has occurred, if, as the Reformers and their confessions have it, faith can never be assent to brute facts, it is precisely biblical criticism and its separation of fact from interpretation, history from significance, occurrence from meaning which asks us to decide, e.g., between the probability or improbability of the revivification of a corpse on the one hand, and on the other the faith of the first apostles that Jesus "was raised for our justification"; to decide between the possibility or impossibility of a tomb emptying itself of its dead and the conviction of the earliest Christian community that "God raised him up, having loosed the pangs of death, because it was not possible for him to be held by it" (Acts 2:24). In short, biblical criticism asks us whether we will hold to the "how," to a particular way of looking at the world, whether it be John's or Paul's or Luther's or our own, or to the "that," the event to which that world view gives the expression. It can never make the decision for us; it can never heighten or lessen the wager, the venture of faith, but it can point to where the wager is made and in that sense radicalize faith. Herein lies the witness or confession of biblical criticism.

Further, biblical criticism makes its confession by pointing to the sovereignty of God. Returning again to the resurrection narratives, scores of

70

biblical interpreters, from the eighteenth-century Wolfenbüttel fragmentist to twentieth-century expositors, have devised any number of solutions by which to explain the rise of faith in the disciples following Jesus' crucifixion. Reimarus suggested that the disciples had spirited Jesus' body away, and after a fifty days' interval which made identification of the corpse impossible, returned to perpetrate the fraud that he had risen. In that same century, the rationalist H. E. G. Paulus (1761-1851) interpreted Jesus' resurrection as revival from a coma followed by a premature burial. A modern American interpreter treats Matthew's narrative in this fashion:

Matthew tells how the eleven disciples went to Galilee, to the mountain to which Jesus had directed them. There they saw him and bowed down before him. . . .

Then he gave them their great commission. . . . They are to go and make disciples of all the heathen, and to teach them to observe all that he has commanded. And he will be with them always, to the very close of the age.

71

That he is to be with them always, to the very end, shows that it is not as a physical presence that he has come back to them, but as a spiritual one. . . . "Their memory of him quickened to a presence." The thing we most crave about our beloved departed is not so much their physical reanimation, but rather just this sense of their living presence with us, in our hearts, in guidance, sympathy, companionship and counsel.[7]

The point to be made here is not that a spiritual presence is set in contrast to a physical presence— every Easter, pulpits echo with talk of "glorified" and "spiritual" bodies and suchlike. It is rather the use to which our commentator puts such a contrast which sets him in the same pew with a Reimarus or a Paulus—assigning the resurrection to the initiative of the disciples. Now, biblical criticism will never be able to go beyond the statement of a Dibelius that "something must have happened." It may try to account for that Easter faith in the personal intimacy which the disciples enjoyed with Jesus during his earthly life and interpret the resurrection appearances in terms of a series of subjective visions, as did Friedrich

Schleiermacher and as does Rudolf Bultmann (1884-   ) on occasion. In the end, however, it will never be able to go beyond establishing the Easter-faith of the disciples, beyond establishing the fact that *they* believed Christ had been raised. But it can tell us where the initiative in all this ought to be laid, whatever our view of the resurrection. It can point to that little verb ἠγέρθη ("he was raised") trumpeted in the first three Gospels as well as in the earliest of all Christian kerygmas (I Cor. 15:1 ff.), every one of which assign the initiative in this act not to the disciples, not even to Jesus (the verb is in the passive!) but to God himself. It can insist that if we must believe in such a thing as a resurrection, we ought to see it as an occurrence which is contingent upon a particular person, place, and period, a contingency which reflects the freedom and sovereignty of One who creates time and times in which faith becomes possibility. And it can tell us that the reason we have Gospels at all is that men were convinced of this contingency and hence of this sovereignty, who believed that the initiative lay with God and not with themselves, believed that God was there before they believed. In this sense too, biblical criticism can make a confession.

But biblical criticism also gives a witness to the vulnerability of faith in this world. When we examine the resurrection accounts in the four Gospels, we can scarcely but agree with Luther's terse comment to the effect that everything has been substantially confused—*omnia immixta*.[8] Among the accounts, no two agree. In Matthew Mary Magdalene and "the other Mary" proceed to the tomb; in Mark Mary Magdalene, Mary the mother of James, and Salome; in Luke Mary Magdalene, Joanna, Mary the mother of James, and other women; in John mention is made only of Mary Magdalene. In Matthew's account the grave is not yet opened when the women appear. In the others the stone is already rolled away. In Matthew an angel announces the resurrection to the women; in Mark "a young man"; and in Luke two men in "dazzling apparel." Matthew records

Jesus as first appearing to the women; in Mark
and Luke no hint is given of such an appearance,
and in John he appears only to Mary Magdalene.
In Matthew and Luke the women inform the
disciples of what they have seen and heard; in
Mark the women are too terrified to speak; in John
no women at all appear to break the news. In
Matthew and John Jesus appears both in Jerusalem and in Galilee; in Mark only in Galilee and
in Luke only in Jerusalem. The earliest Christian
kerygma in I Cor. 15 raises further questions.
There it is said that Christ "was raised on the
third day in accordance with the scriptures," yet
there is no biblical passage anywhere which can
be construed in such a sense. Jesus is further reported as appearing first to Peter—an appearance
which is alluded to in Luke, but only after the
Emmaus incident (Luke 24:13 ff.) ; James is also
numbered among the witnesses, but about him
the Gospels say nothing. Finally, in that ancient
kerygma, there is no mention of the empty tomb.
These are only problems which encounter us upon

a quick perusal of the pericopes. There are others, more troublesome, which deal with the role which legendary, apologetic, cultic-liturgical, and polemical tendencies might have played in the various accounts as well as in their apocryphal counterparts. Now, many of these problems are capable of some solution. But the old foolish stunt of shutting off all the avenues until only one remains —belief in the resurrection—is doomed to failure. Whether the solution advanced be the harmonizing of an earlier orthodoxy whose theory of Scripture allowed no room for divergent traditions, whether it be the psychologistic interpretation of nineteenth-century Protestantism, or perhaps a modern skepticism in reverse, which out of fear before possible critical results raptures faith in the resurrection out of all interest in its possible historical occasion, all of them finally shatter on the cold, hard residue of the contradictory, the discrepant, the absurd which offers itself to natural explanation and to faith alike. For when the biblical critic has completed his analysis of the ac-

counts, furnished his solution, and put down his
tools, only two options are left to the hearer—to
quote Albert Schweitzer, perhaps, "It is . . . Jesus
as spiritually arisen within men, who is significant
for our time," [9] or W. H. Auden:

He is the Way.
Follow Him through the Land of Unlikeness;
You will see rare beasts, and have unique adventures.

He is the Truth.
Seek Him in the Kingdom of Anxiety;
You will come to a great city that has expected your
    return for years.

He is the Life.
Love Him in the World of the Flesh;
And at your marriage all its occasions shall dance
    for joy.[10]

And if the hearer chooses to believe that God
raised Jesus from the dead, then it is biblical
criticism which has opened his eyes to the character
of his decision, a decision without refuge.

There is no dogma which can comfort him,

whether that dogma is the result of some rational, "natural" theology, or the outcome of a logical systematization of ideas gleaned from the Bible itself. For this decision has nothing whatever to do with that purely formal and purely human attitude we sometimes call belief in dogma. It is God who is to be believed here; a man can only understand or subordinate himself to a dogma. There is no experience to which he can turn. There is nothing within, nothing native to him which can provide him any kind of basis for legitimizing what he has decided to believe. And if he should attempt to certify the word which he trusts by his own longing for immortality, he has only made himself the object of his faith, for he has credited his own longing with the initiative for an act for which he wanted God and God alone to be responsible! There is no institution which can give him shelter. Gerhard Ebeling, presently of the University of Zürich, once stated that the papal encyclical *Divino afflante spiritu,* issued by Pius XII in 1943, to the effect that the authenticity of the Vulgate

78

is to be understood not in any critical but only in a juridical sense, did not bring agreement between Protestants and Catholics one step nearer. On the contrary, Ebeling contended, it merely indicated that the Roman Church had become so convinced of its absolute authority that it could afford to be magnanimous in regard to the problems of biblical criticism.[11] But that was fourteen years ago! And although liberal Catholics in attendance at recent sessions of the Vatican Council may require Protestants about to pick up their spirits, there is a tide of progressive thought in contemporary Catholicism which not even a thousand Holy Offices and Ottavianis can eventually stem. When cracks appear in the wall of that one institution which few dared to dream would be anything else than the bulwark of obscurantism to all eternity (a situation, by the way, for which Protestant scholasticism must bear its share of the responsibility), how can Protestants ever hope to find refuge for their faith in a church which they have not yet troubled adequately to define?

"There's no hidin' place down here." The witness of biblical criticism is that faith must stand upon its own two feet, without guarantees, solitary and alone, ambiguous to the naked eye, vulnerable to criticism, to the contradictions, discrepancies, and absurdities, struggling for understanding, and, once in a blue moon, perhaps in some sudden blaze of light, perceiving that its own paradox answers to the paradox of human existence, but in the end admitting to its vulnerability and ambiguity and nonetheless confessing "I believe . . . in Jesus Christ, His only Son, our Lord; Who was . . . crucified, dead, and buried; He descended into hell; The third day He rose again from the dead."

There is scarcely a volume, essay, or argument which has had such telling effect on many a contemporary theologian as has Luther's sermon on the Canaanite woman in Matthew 15. Somehow, that one sermon has provided him the clue to whatever it means to be a Christian. Listen to a few random lines:

This was written to comfort and teach us all to know how deeply God hides his grace for us and how we should cling, not to our feelings or thoughts about him, but strictly to his Word. . . . For this reason our heart must turn aside from such feelings and with firm faith in God's Word seize and cling to the Yes deep and hidden beneath and beyond the No, just as this woman, and give God his due when he judges us. Then we have won him and caught him in his own words.[12]

It is precisely this aspect of the vulnerability of faith, of its exposure to the ambiguity of history and historical existence to which biblical criticism witnesses. And that exposure, that vulnerability in turn is nothing but the reverse side of the certainty of our salvation by grace through faith alone. Coming as it does to the biblical texts with no schema of its own, having no option but to take its place with other historical study and philosophy in virtually the same struggle to discover the nature and proper use of method, passing through the same shadows and dangers as its sister disciplines, verifying only what can be verified, demonstrating only what can be demonstrated, separating, abstracting specific data from out of that total context of the historic event to which faith is related; it places the hearer or reader before the fundamental question—whether he will believe without searching for guarantees. And the more radical the criticism, the less there remains to be demonstrated, the more burning the question. In answer then to the attitudes of anxiety and optimism, biblical criticism deserves its freedom, for without destroying or supporting faith, it nevertheless aids faith in retaining its integrity. Hence to struggle on behalf of the one is to struggle on behalf of the other.

It is time now to put the period. You have seen that the discipline referred to as biblical criticism has not been foisted upon the church by the chance skepticism of a few, rather, as Franz Overbeck (1837-1905) once said, that it has "rolled down upon it through the centuries," [13] and, that it is not a matter of indifference because of the task to which it addresses itself—the exposition of the biblical text. You have been exposed to at least one answer to the attitudes of anxiety and optimism in the face of such criticism, that is, that it can neither destroy nor support, but rather confesses, witnesses, to the place where faith must make its wager and for this reason deserves its freedom. Two alternatives confront you. Either you will attempt to make good what you believe Protestantism has failed to do, to salvage something from the burning by way of a dogma, a religion of experience, or an institution, or you will let burn everything that will burn and without reservation wait for what proves to be unburnable. Until now, a few Protestant denominations have officially chosen the first alternative. The documents they append to their historic confessions make this amply clear. The various crises recently developing within these sectors of Protestantism result from such an official stance and its variance with a practice begun early in the church's life and to which I believe the Reformation gospel of faith alone gave theological justification. If you choose the first alternative, you perhaps need not change your habit of life beyond fending off what comes from the outside. If you choose the second, you will have to apply yourself to the task of interpretation, whether in the pulpit or out of it, with an industry and seriousness which will make whatever else you do in your ministry an avocation. The problems of textual, literary, and historical criticism, and the greater problem of actualizing the biblical message will in a sense become your daily bread. Further, you will face the inevitable heartbreak which results from trodding a path which takes you through bitter crises and bewildering debates which appear to end only in weakness and collapse. Finally, you will be judged heterodox, for it is totally impossible to carry on biblical research in light of the interpretation of Scripture which many have officially received, unalterably fixed in their documents, and required of their ordinands. I invite you to choose this second alternative, but whichever you choose, make up your mind about this—there will never be an end to criticism, good or bad, as long as man has a brain and life to use it, as long as the Gospel requires the "preparation of the intelligence." But to him, "the only wise God be glory for evermore through Jesus Christ! Amen."

GLOSSARY OF TERMS

allegorical interpretation—a treatment of the biblical text as metaphor, either for the purpose of accommodating it to church dogma or of demonstrating its relevance to daily life. In the Middle Ages it comprised one of the fourfold senses of Scripture: *quid credas allegoria*—"the allegorical sense teaches what you believe."

apocalyptic—most generally referring to Jewish and Christian writings which assay to "unveil" the future for the purpose of disclosing to the reader the comfort of a better day.

apocryphal—"hidden," "secret," of unknown origin, spurious.

apologetic—of the "defense" of religion.

Arminians—members of a school in Reformed theology named after Jacob Arminius (1560-1609), who asserted man's freedom over against the unconditional predestination of Calvinism.

canon—"bar," "ruler," hence standard or rule. Used of the Christian Scriptures.

Christology—the study of the person and work of Christ.

collated—"placed," arranged in proper order.

commentary—a volume devoted to the interpretation of one or several books of the Bible.

comparative religion—the description of religions as phenomena accessible to scientific research.

cultic-liturgical—pertaining to formal worship, separate from the piety of daily life with an existence and structure of its own.

Divino afflante spiritu—an encyclical letter issued by Pope Pius XII in 1943 on the promotion of biblical studies, commencing with the words, "Inspired by the Divine Spirit."

dogma—"opinion," belief, hence a tenet of faith, a binding decree.

dogmatism—used of the penchant among second-generation Reformers for transforming the dynamic and fluid ideas of their spiritual fathers into fixed systems.

enlightenment—an era beginning in the seventeenth and culminating in the eighteenth century, marked by confidence in scientific method, thus in human reason. Its motto à la Immanuel Kant: "Have courage to use your own reason!"

epistemological—pertaining to the study of how we know what we know.

exegesis—the methodical uncovering of the intention of the author of a biblical text.

expositor—the scholar responsible for exegeting and/or making contemporary a specific biblical book or text.

extant—"visible," existent, available.

extra ecclesiam—outside the church.

formal principle—the principle of the sole sufficiency of Scripture in matters of faith and life.

gnostic—a "knower," *i.e.* a devotee of one of the great second-century systems which taught deliverance from man's body-prison by means of knowledge communicated by a Redeemer figure or other heavenly message. Applicable to Marcion only in the widest sense, due to his emphasis upon salvation by faith.

heretical—belonging to a school of "thought," a sect departing from authorized teaching.

heremeneutical—referring to the science or art of interpretation, specifically, to that branch of theology which illumines the exegetical mode of operation.

historiography—the writing of history.

Holy Office—synonymous with "Inquisition," a tribunal of the Roman Catholic hierarchy established in the thirteenth century for the trial and disposition of heresies.

humanism—a term applied to the fifteenth and sixteenth centuries—an age of invention and discovery, of reformation, nationalism, and the rise of the middle class—marked by the study of antiquity as stimulated by the penetration of Greek-Arabic literature to the Latin west.

integrity—in an "unimpaired condition"; correctness, genuineness.

justification—in this essay used simply of God's gift of Jesus Christ by which everything he is and has becomes mine.

kerygma—the English transliteration of a Greek term denoting "good tidings" (i.e. of Jesus Christ).

legend—a "saying," religious and edifying rather than historical in character.

lexicographical—pertaining to the examination of words and their meanings.

Loci—referring to Philip Melanchthon's *Loci Communes* of 1521, in which the evangelical principles of the German Reformation were set forth in topical fashion.

modernism—under this title, Pope Pius X in 1907 condemned attempts within Roman Catholicism to apply modern theories of knowledge and historical criticism to biblical studies, the doctrine of the church, and Christology.

monograph—a volume devoted to a single theological problem or question.

myth—a "tale," fable, or an ideology. Occasionally used of that biblical mode of address by which the divine is described as human.

obscurantism—an attitude hostile to the progress or spread of knowledge.

orthodoxy—a period in Protestantism, opening with the formulation of comprehensive confessions and in which, by means of medieval scholasticism, the great dogmatic systems emerged.

Pentateuch—the first five books of the Old Testament.

pericope—a biblical passage singled out (literally, "cut around") for purposes of examination or for reading at public worship. In the so-called "liturgical" communions of Christendom, the scriptural lessons and sermon follow pericopes from both Testaments which are assigned to each Sunday of the year.

philological—pertaining to the study of literature; in a wide sense including etymology, grammar, criticism, literary and linguistic history, etc.

polemical—of the "offensive" on behalf of religion.

rationalism—a world view espousing reason as man's highest spiritual and religious capacity.

Reformers—the term applied to the fathers of Protestantism: Luther, Zwingli, Calvin, etc.

romanticist—in general referring to anyone who finds the source of certainty in inner experience, feeling, and instinct.

scholasticism—a type of theology intent on venerating ancient teachers and texts. In the narrower sense, the theology of the Middle Ages which sought to establish a comprehensive system by way of combining Augustinianism with Aristotelianism.

secular—of the worldly or temporal as opposed to the spiritual or eternal.

skepticism—originally used of philosophical schools which asserted nothing positively. In Christian circles applied to any view proceeding from a denial of the miraculous or divine.

Socinians—members of a sect named after Faustus Socinus (1539-1604) who emphasized a religion of reason as the criterion for biblical authority.

Syllabus of Errors—a compendium of eighty "errors" published by Pope Pius XI in 1864, in which liberal, rationalistic, and naturalistic views regarding modern national, social, and religious life were condemned.

synoptic—referring to the first three Gospels in the New Testament.

textual variants—the various alternate readings of a given biblical passage.

transmission—used of handing down the biblical contents from one generation to another.

the Vulgate—Jerome's revision of the Old Latin texts, made in 383-400 at the behest of Pope Damasus and dubbed *vulgata* ("commonly diffused") at the end of the Middle Ages.

NOTES

Origins

1. *Offenbarungsglaube und historische Wissenchaft*, in Gerhard Ebeling, *Word and Faith*, translated by James W. Leitch (Philadelphia: Fortress Press, 1963), p. 19.
2. *Es stehet geschrieben*, in Ebeling, *op. cit.*, pp. 19-20.
3. Werner Keller, *The Bible As History*, translated by William Neil (New York: William Morrow and Co., 1956).
4. *Und die Bibel hat doch Recht—Forscher beweisen die historische Wahrheit* (7te Auflage; Düsseldorf: Econverlag, 1956).
5. Keller, *The Bible As History*, p. xxv.
6. *Encyclopaedia Britannica* (11th ed.; New York: Encyclopaedia Britannica, Inc., 1911), XVII, 692.
7. The Epistle of Barnabas, ix. 8. Author's translation.
8. B. Smalley, *The Study of the Bible in the Middle Ages* (2nd ed.; New York: Philosophical Library, 1952), p. 166.
9. Hartmann Grisar, *Martin Luthers Leben und sein Werk* (2te Auflage, Freiburg im Breisgau: Herder, 1927), p. 236. Author's translation.
10. *Die Deutsche Bibel, D. Martin Luthers Werke, Kritische Gesamtausgabe* (Weimar: Hermann Böhlaus Nachfolger, 1883 f.), 7, 344, 17 f.; 384, 9 ff.; 386, 22 f; 404, 1 ff. Hereafter, references to the Weimar Edition

of Luther's works will read simply WA; WA, DB (*Die Deutsche Bibel*) or WA, TR (*Tischreden*). All translations are the author's.

11. *WA, DB* 7, 404, 29-30.
12. *WA* 17, II, 471, 11; 47, 340, 32; *WA, DB* 6, 203.
13. *Fragments from Reimarus,* translated from the German by G. E. Lessing, edited by Charles Voysey (London: Williams and Norgate, 1879), p. 115.

Task

1. *WA* 27, 492, 11 f.; 10, I, 71, 1-10.
2. *WA* 9, 518, 17 f.
3. *The Loci Communes of Philip Melanchthon,* with a critical introduction by the translator, Charles Leander Hill (Boston: Meador Publishing Co., 1944), pp. 175, 176, 177.
4. Wilhelm Wrede, *Das Messiasgeheimnis in den Evangelien* (Göttingen: Vandenhoeck und Ruprecht, 1901).
5. Albert Schweitzer, *The Quest of the Historical Jesus,* translated by W. Montgomery (New York: The Macmillan Co., 1958), Ch. XIX.
6. Ernst Käsemann, "Das Problem des historischen Jesus," *Zeitschrift für Theologie und Kirche,* 51. Jahrgang, 1954, p. 150. Author's translation.
7. Ernest Renan, *The Memoirs of Ernest Renan,* translated by J. Lewis May (London: Geoffrey Bles, 1935), pp. 174-205.
8. Martin Dibelius, *Jesus,* translated by Charles B. Hedrick and Frederick C. Grant (Philadelphia: The Westminster Press, 1949), p. 141.
9. Søren Kierkegaard, *Philosophical Fragments,* translated by David F. Swenson (Princeton: Princeton University Press, 1936), p. 79.

10. Karl Barth, *The Epistle to the Romans*, translated from the 6th ed. by Edwyn C. Hoskyns (New York: Oxford University Press, 1933), p. 1.

Witness

1. Barth, *The Epistle to the Romans*, p. 8.
2. *The Gospel According to St. Luke, The International Critical Commentary*, ed. A. Plummer, S. R. Driver, and C. A. Briggs (5th ed.; Edinburgh: T. and T. Clark, 1922) pp. 57-58. Author's translation of Greek words in text.
3. Barth, *loc. cit.*
4. *WA, TR* 5, Nos. 5468, 5677.
5. *WA* 36, 500, 28-501, 10.
6. *The Gospel According to St. Mark, The Interpreter's Bible* (Nashville: Abingdon Press, 1951), VII, 912.
7. Edgar J. Goodspeed, *A Life of Jesus* (New York: Harper & Row, 1950), pp. 225-26.
8. *WA* 17, I, 178, 7; 179, 1.
9. Schweitzer, *op. cit.*, p. 399.
10. From "For the Time Being," in *The Collected Poetry of W. H. Auden* (New York: Random House, 1945), p. 466.
11. Ebeling, *op. cit.*, pp. 52-55, n. 1.
12. *WA* 17, II, 203, 15-18, 31-35.
13. Franz Overbeck, *Über Entstehung und Recht einer rein historischen Betrachtung der neutestamentlich Schriften in der Theologie* (Basel: Schweighauserische Verlagsbuchhandlung, 1871), p. 4.